WILDFLOWER PHOTOGRAPHY

GETTING FROM "THAT'S NICE" TO "WOW"!

Photography and Text

By

Al Lodwick

First Edition 2016

ISBN 978-1537199818

DEDICATION

To Ann Lodwick, my wife and best friend, whose love and shared interests have supported me for almost 39 years.

INTRODUCTION

Shortly after someone gets a new camera with lots of adjustable settings, they usually want to take exceptional pictures of flowers. Quite often, the camera has a setting that looks like a flower, hinting that you should use this setting for flowers. While you will be able to focus very close to the subject, the results are often disappointing because of distracting backgrounds. The method that I am going to show you makes very limited use of that close focus setting.

Inherent in any optical lens is what is known as a depth of field. The simplest demonstration of this is a pair of reading glasses. The magnification will help you see more clearly but the object you are looking at must be not too close and not too far away. This is the depth of field. The depth of field varies greatly with the magnification (power) of the lens. A wide-angle lens has a tremendous depth of field. It is the lens of choice for photographers wishing to show both a close-up of a flower and the mountain five miles distant in sharp focus. At the other end of the array of lenses are the extreme telephotos that will have only a few inches of depth of field. This is particularly true when they are used near their minimum focusing distance. A wide-angle lens will have its minimum focusing distance measured in fractions of an inch. An extreme telephoto lens may have a minimum focusing distance of more than ten feet. You need to keep this in mind when you are deciding what lens to purchase next. I have owned many lenses of varying focal length and have settled on a camera with a built-in wide-angle to extreme telephoto. The latest anti-shake computer programs built into newer cameras are rendering tripods obsolete. Some of the photos in this book were taken with the equivalent of a 2000 mm lens and none of them were taken with a tripod. This book will demonstrate how to use a combination of a hand-held, long telephoto lens in conjunction with a photo editing program to give a final product of a flower picture that you will be proud to show your viewers.

All of the pictures in this book were taken with a zoom lens at the focal length that gave the minimum focusing distance from my vantage point. This is important because this gives the maximum in-camera magnification possible in every situation. Another thing that you must consider in your choice of cameras is the number of megapixels available to record your image. The technique being taught here requires some extreme cropping. The more megapixels you have to work with, the sharper your finished product will appear.

The text will refer to The Rule of Thirds. This is mainly applicable to landscape photography but many apply it to all types of pictures. It simply states that there should be three areas in each photograph that draw your attention. One example of this rule is to have something attractive in the foreground, the middle-ground and the background. Some of the examples will adhere to this rule while others will break it. Where the rule is broken it will be because the subject fills so much of the picture that there is no room for anything else. I have found that viewers respond very well to pictures where the subject seems to explode from its surroundings.

The first six pictures will take you step-by-step through the process from the time the image is taken from the camera until the image is ready for printing. Each of the other pages shows the image as it came from the camera and the finished product. Additional commentary is included about each picture's special situations. All the photos in the book are printed at 300 dots per inch (DPI).

You can utilize this technique whether you are walking in a wilderness, visiting a botanical garden or have a bouquet of flowers set up in an apartment. As with any other skill you will improve with practice, practice and more practice.

Al Lodwick
Prescott, Arizona
August 2016

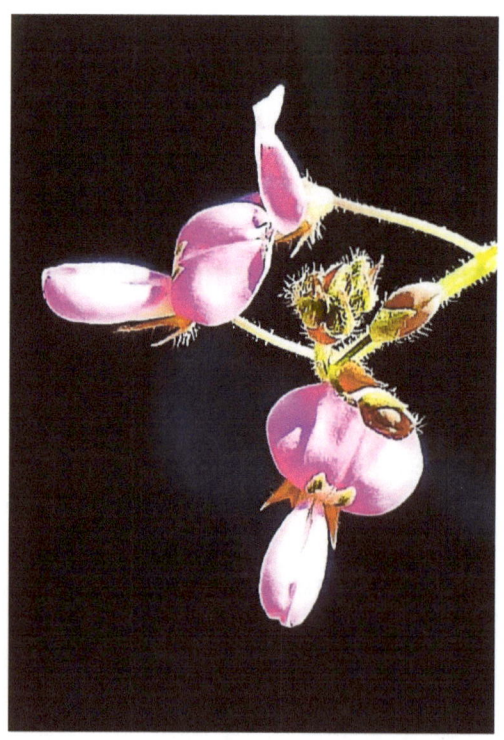

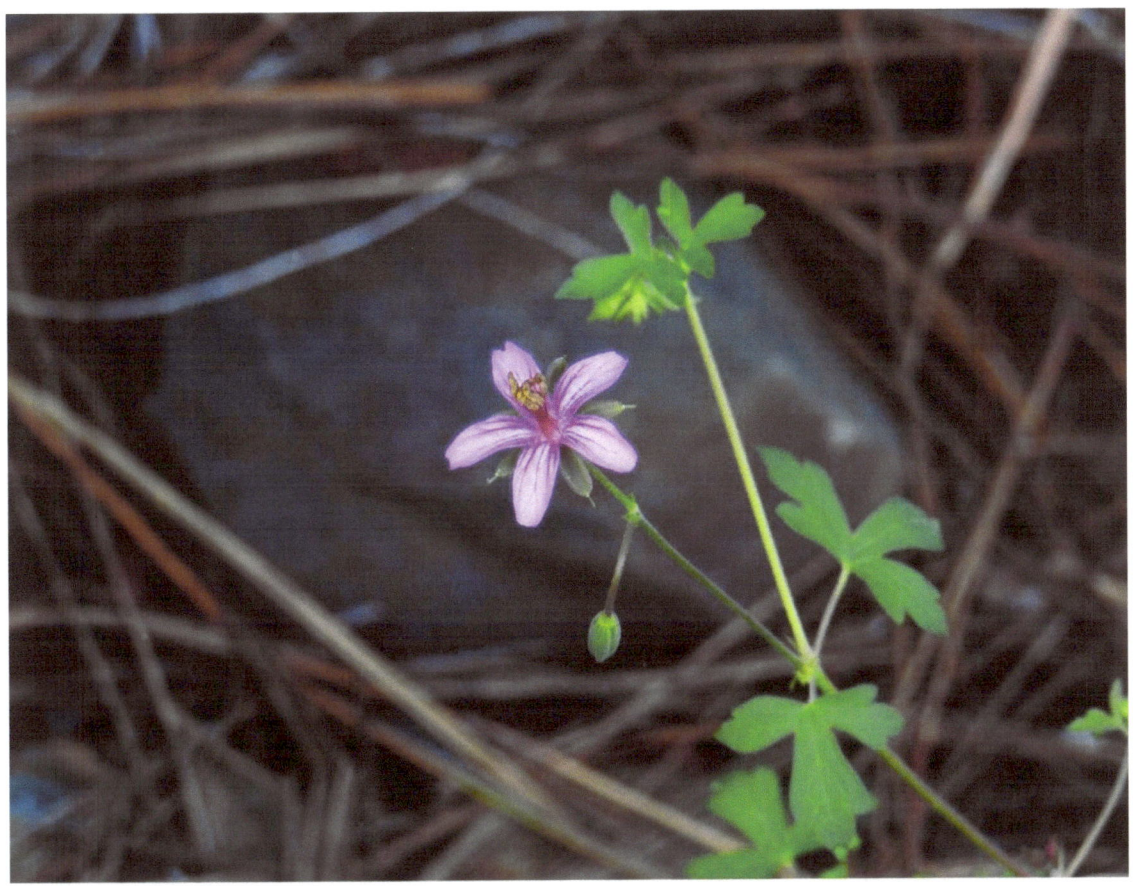

This is a Pineywoods Geranium. It was taken during a walk in the woods. Notice how the flower is against a plain, dark background. I prefer to move around to find the best background possible and to not harm other plants in doing so. Sometimes you will be forced to use a light-colored background. We will discuss how to work with that.

For equipment, I use a camera with a fixed-mount, zoom lens. I recommend getting the longest zoom and the largest number of megapixels that you can afford. The longest zoom will give you minimal depth of field allowing the background to be out of focus. The large number of megapixels will give you maximum clarity when you make an extreme enlargement.

This is the picture as it came out of the camera. Over the next five pages, you will see what can be done with a photo editing program on your computer to make your pictures stand out from the competition.

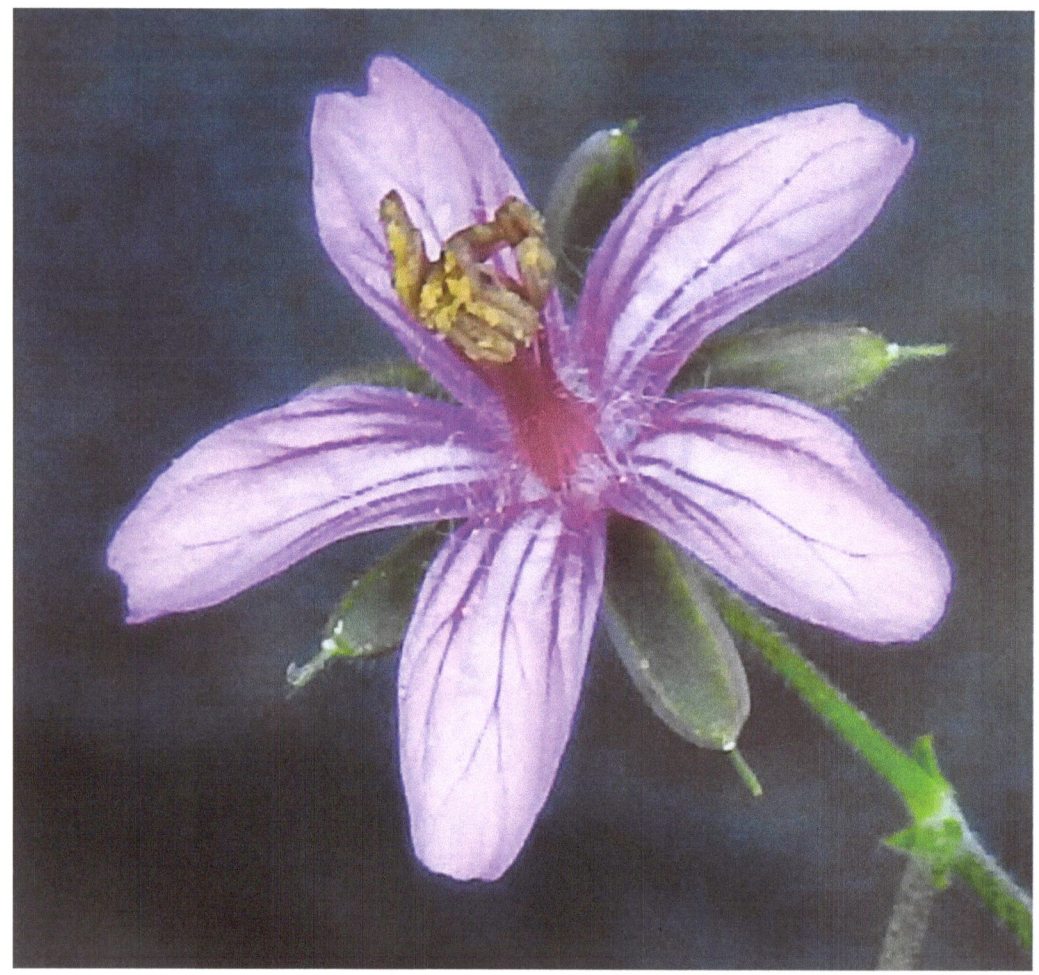

This is the same Pineywoods Geranium that was shown on the previous page. It has now been cropped using a photo editing program. One of the main things that you want to do is to have the picture filled with your subject. Generally, you should conform to the rules of composition for a pleasing picture. One of these is to have a foreground, a middle-ground and a background. Here the purple and gold parts form the foreground and the subject of the picture. The green plant parts form a slightly out-of-focus middle-ground. This conveys a sense of depth and reality to the picture. The dark, gray rock in the original picture has been transformed into a very dark background. I seldom use the choice in the editing program that will lighten the shadows. I want them dark! This causes the subject to pop out of the background.

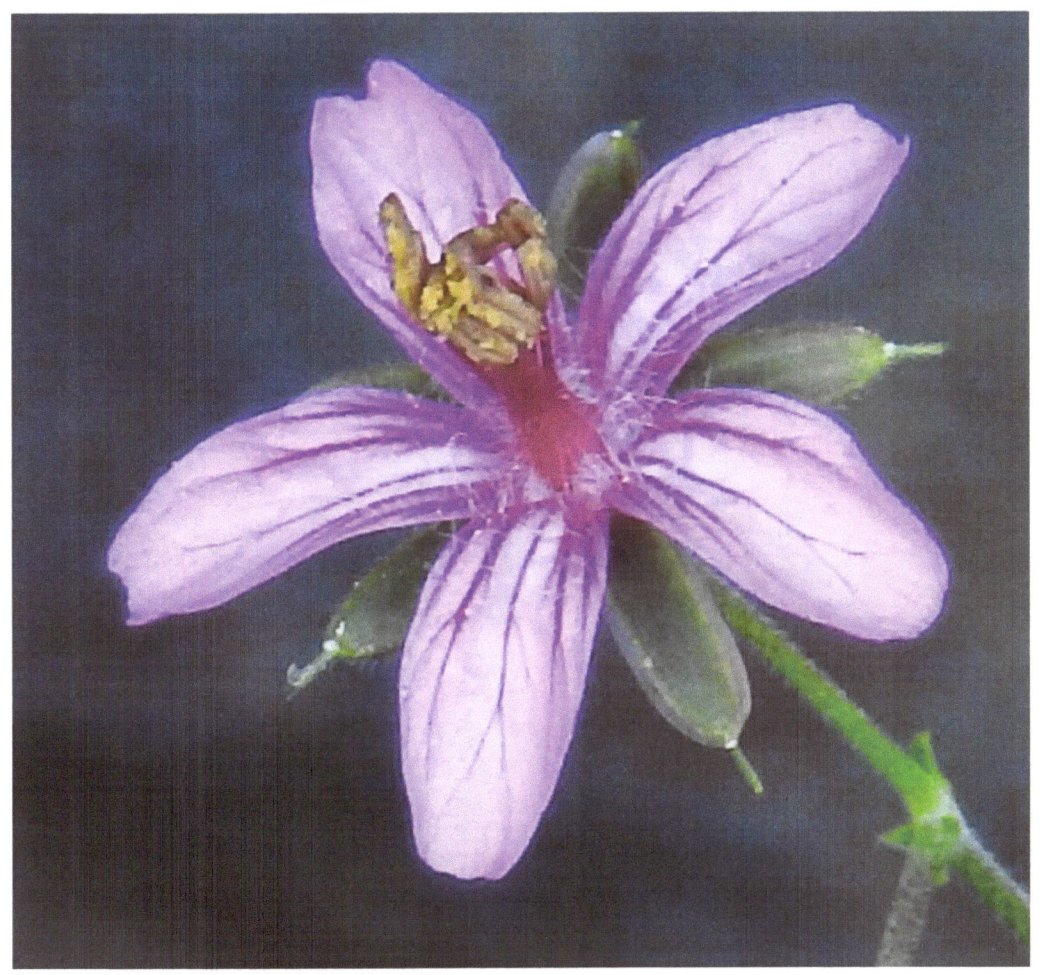

This modification of the picture illustrates something that is purely subjective to the person doing the editing, As mentioned previously, I rarely lighten the shadows. However, I did darken the highlights. My editing program had a slider button that allows me to darken these quite slowly. I often overshoot in this darkening mode and then back off a little.

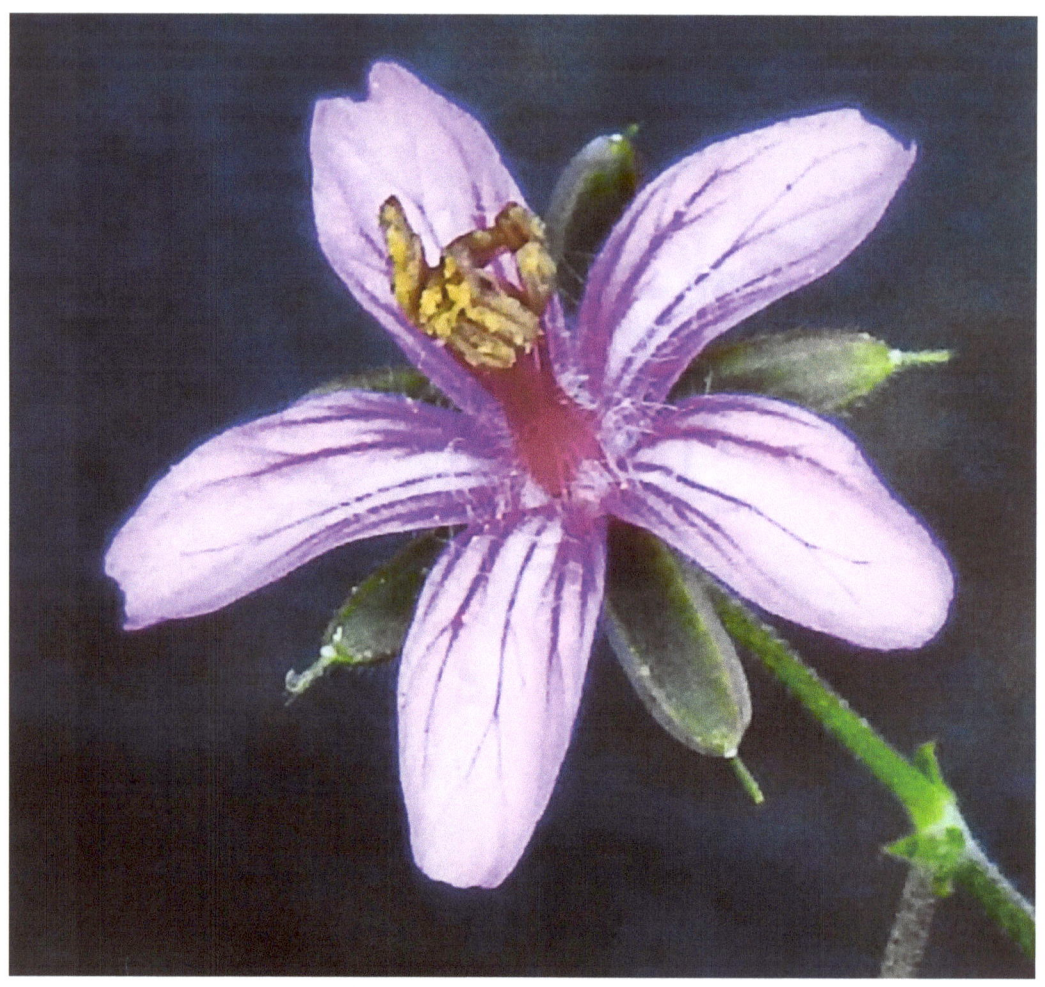

There is also a slider button to lighten or darken the mid-tones. I usually prefer to darken these also to get more saturated colors.

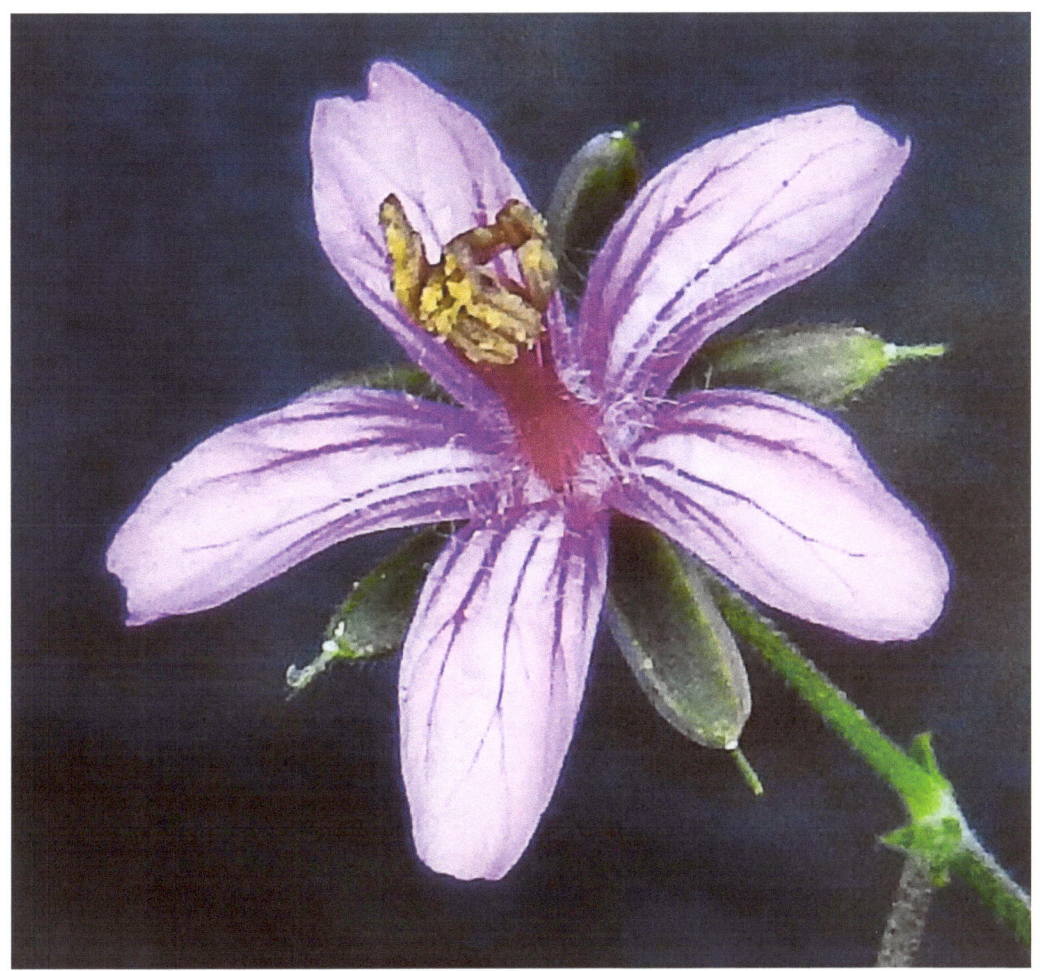

Yet another slider button will allow you to sharpen the picture. You must be cautious with this button because over-sharpening will lead to little white speckles appearing all over the picture.

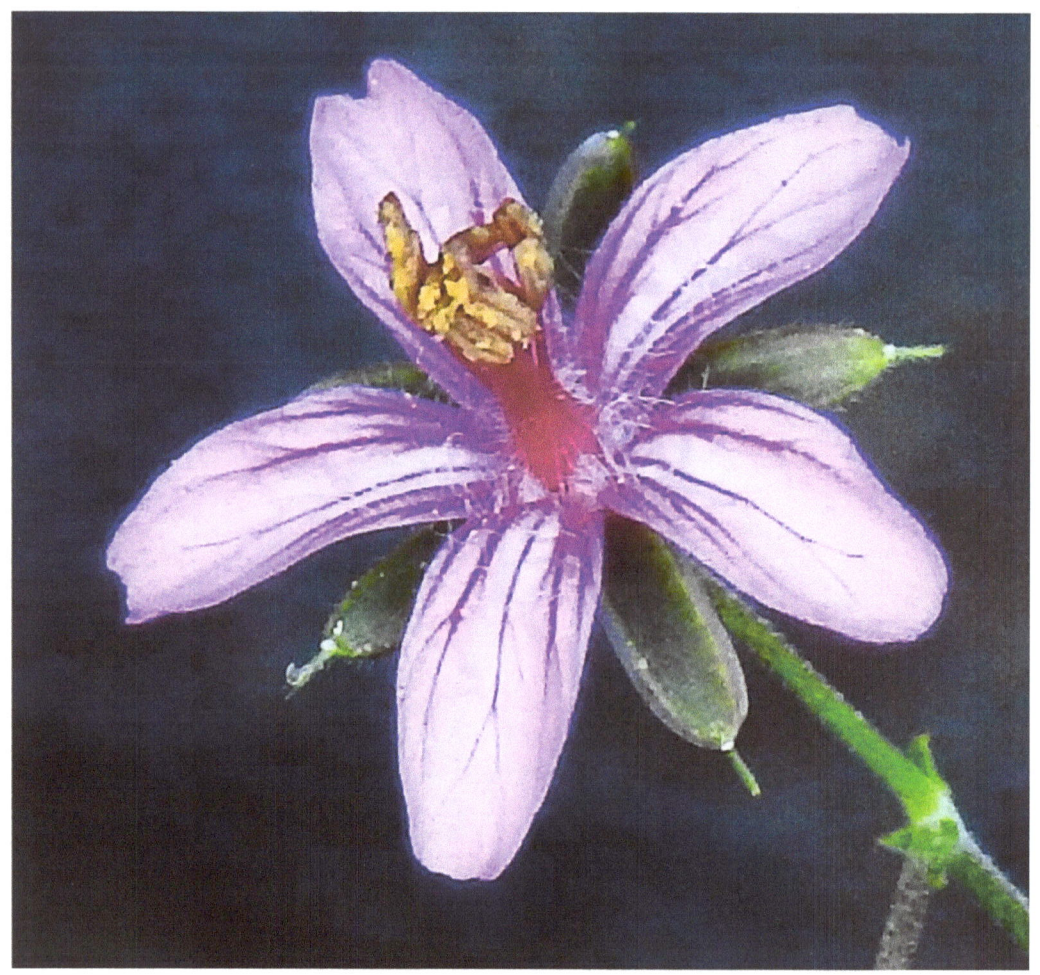

When I started in photography, all that I could afford was black and white film. When color film became affordable, it was amazing to see everything in color. The characteristics of the negative film and the positive color prints led to extremely saturated colors. Ever since then, I have the feeling that saturated colors are the way that things are supposed to be. My editing program has a button to add, "Saturated Film Effect". I almost always click this button once on every picture. Be cautious here. Clicking the button twice may make the picture unrecognizable.

The remainder of the book will consist of before and after pictures to further illustrate techniques.

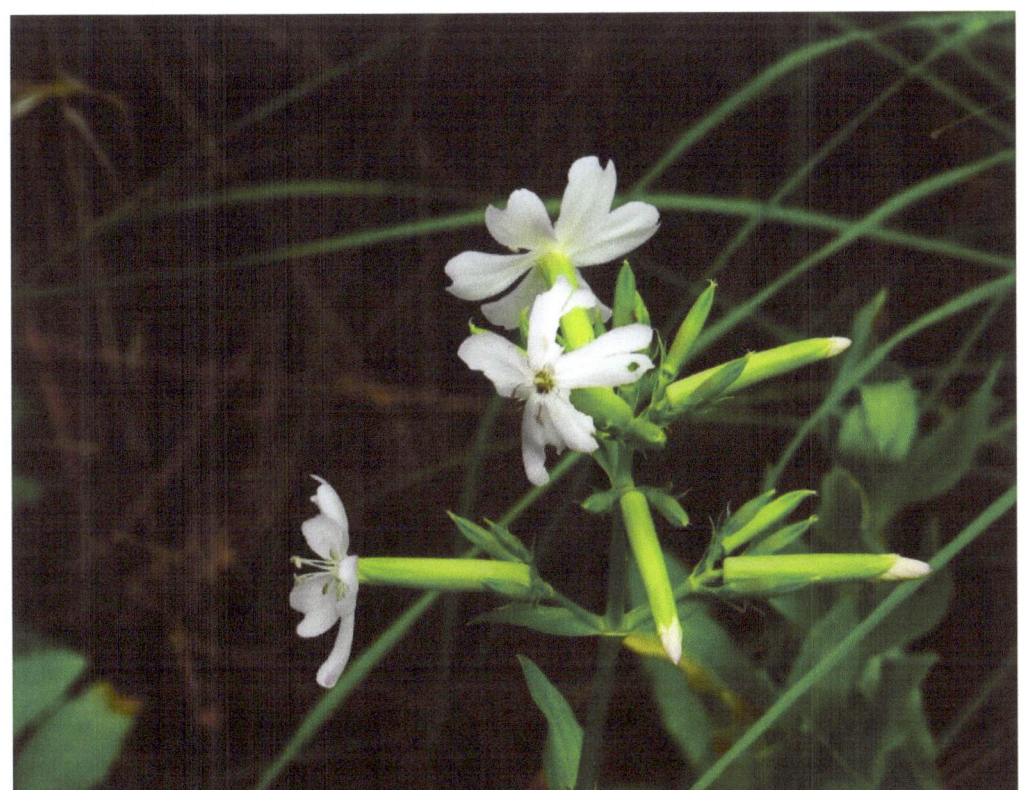

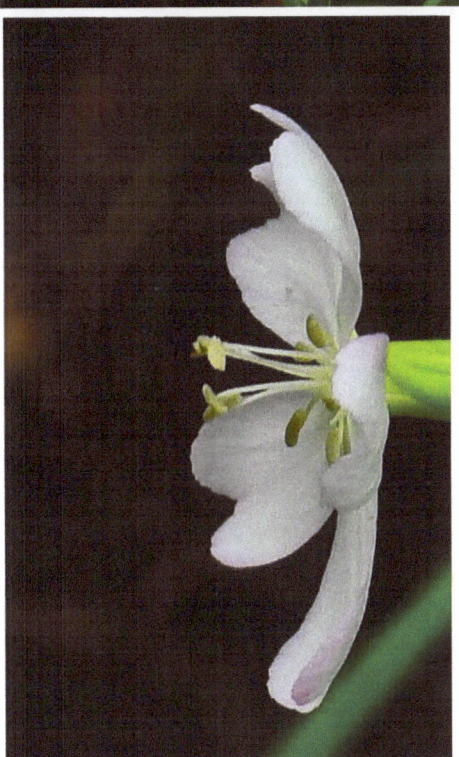

This picture of a Phlox illustrates the value of having as many megapixels as you can afford. The more pixels you have in a given area, the sharper the picture will be when enlarged.

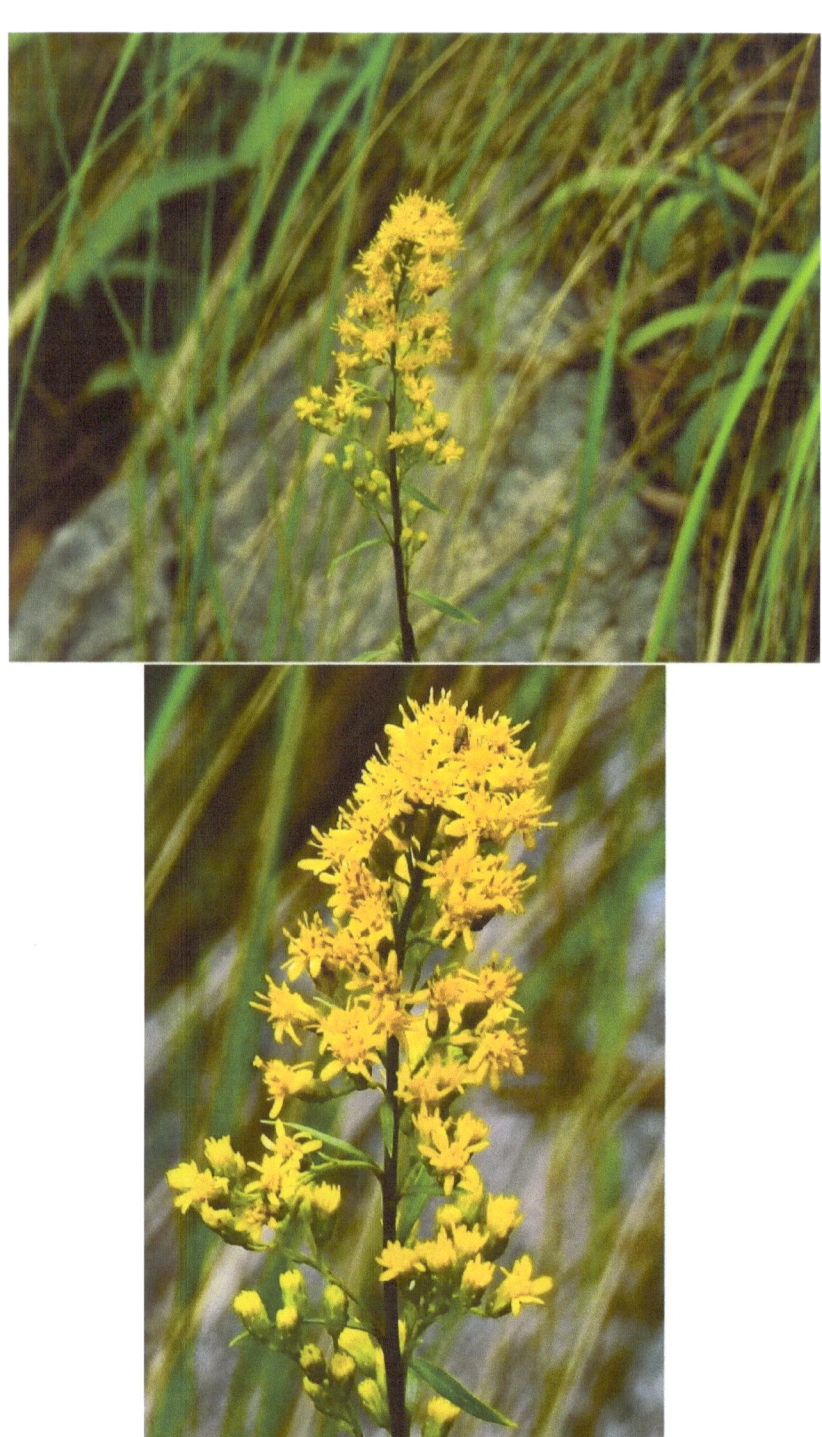

I do not usually try to alter the contrast of a picture. However, it was necessary in this picture of a Goldenrod to do so. The viewer's eyes tend to go to light areas. Decreasing the contrast made the light background less distracting. In turn, this makes the light-colored subject stand out.

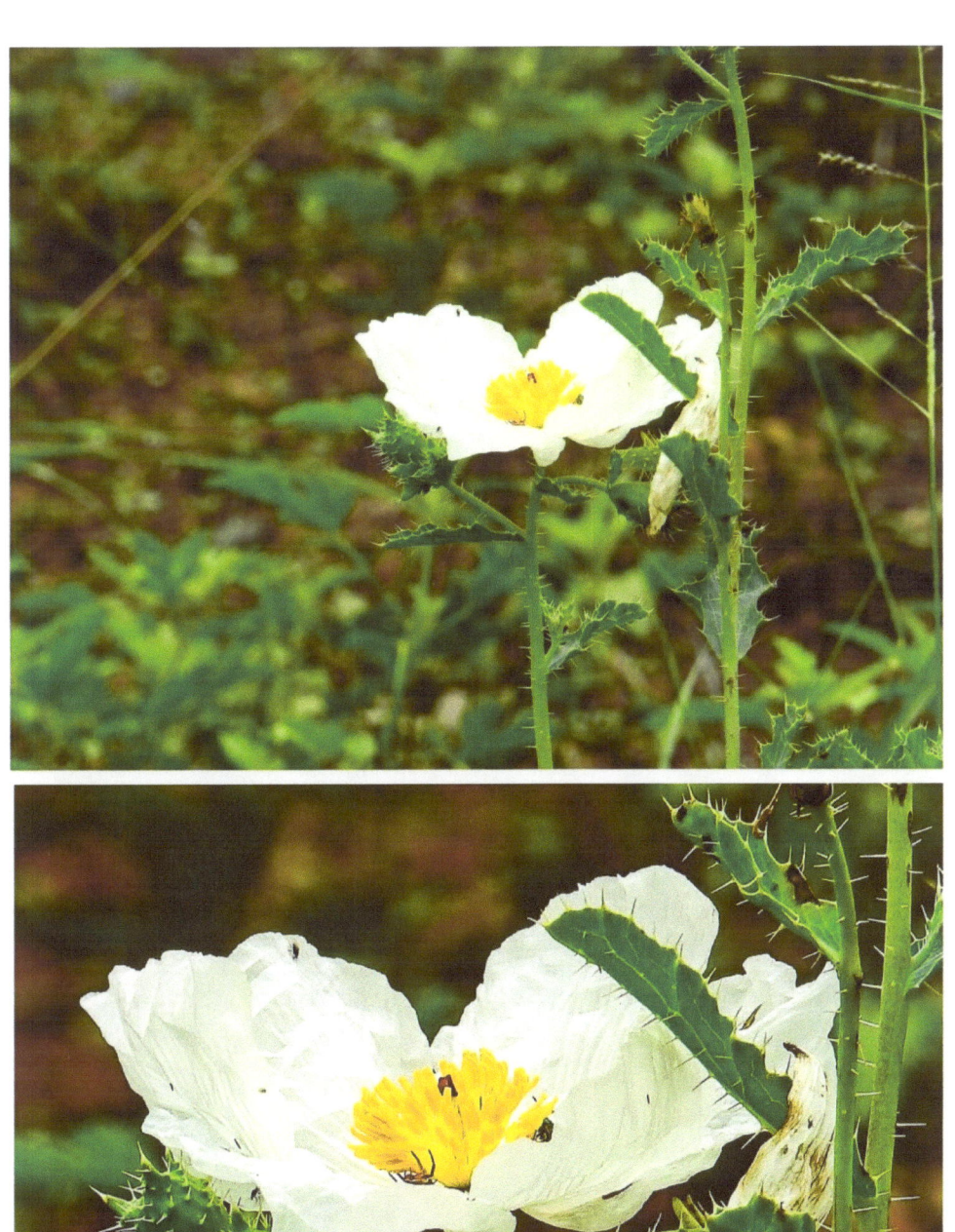

There was no way to get a picture of this Prickly Poppy without the green leaf in front of it. So I used the bud on the opposite side to balance the greens. The in and out of focus green areas with the sharp prickles and the spider near the center lend a sense of danger to an otherwise bland picture.

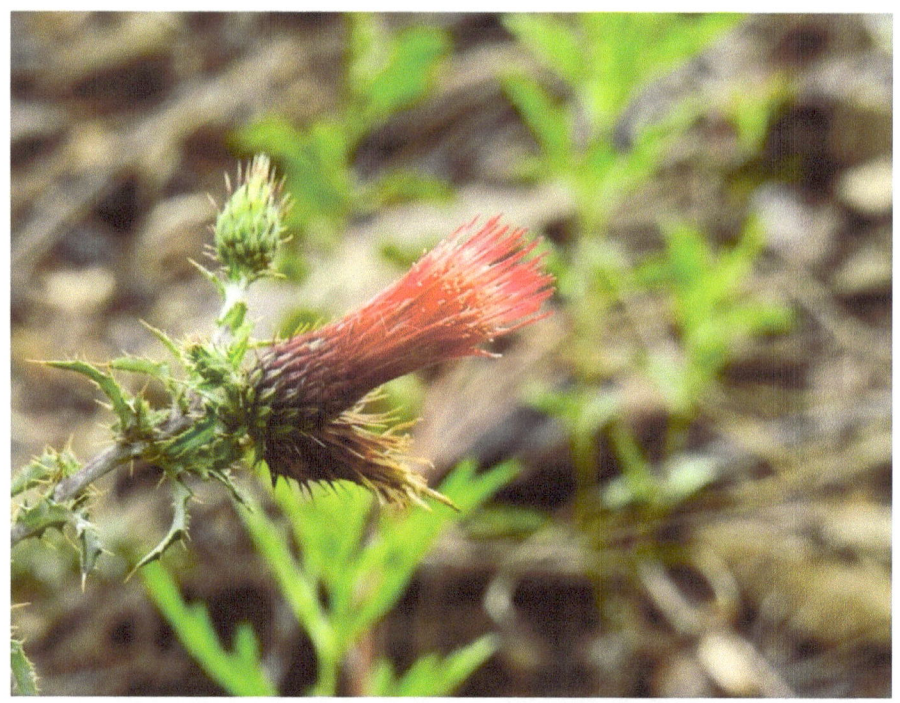

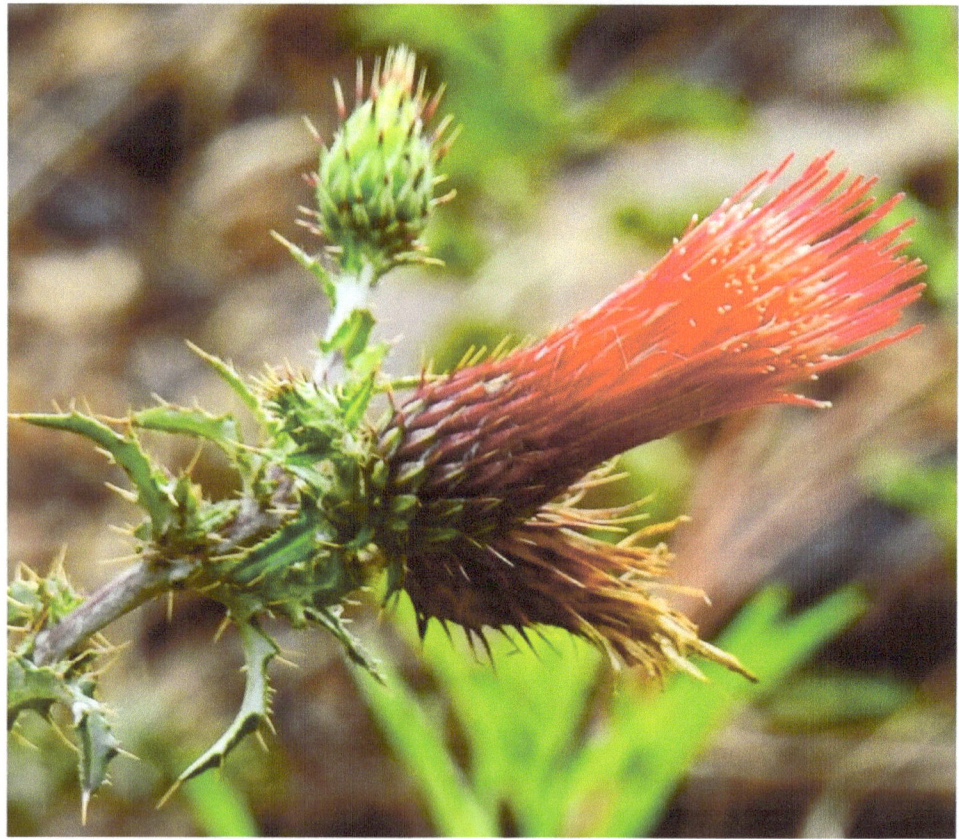

The red of this Arizona Thistle presents a challenge for most cameras, particularly in bright light. Use the exposure compensation control, if you have one, on your camera to darken the picture between 1 and 2 f-stops to lessen the glare.

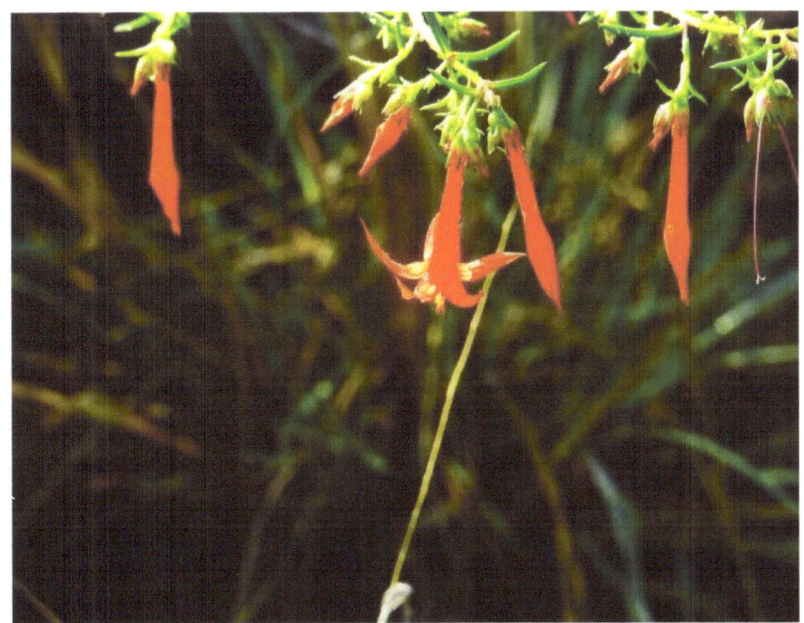

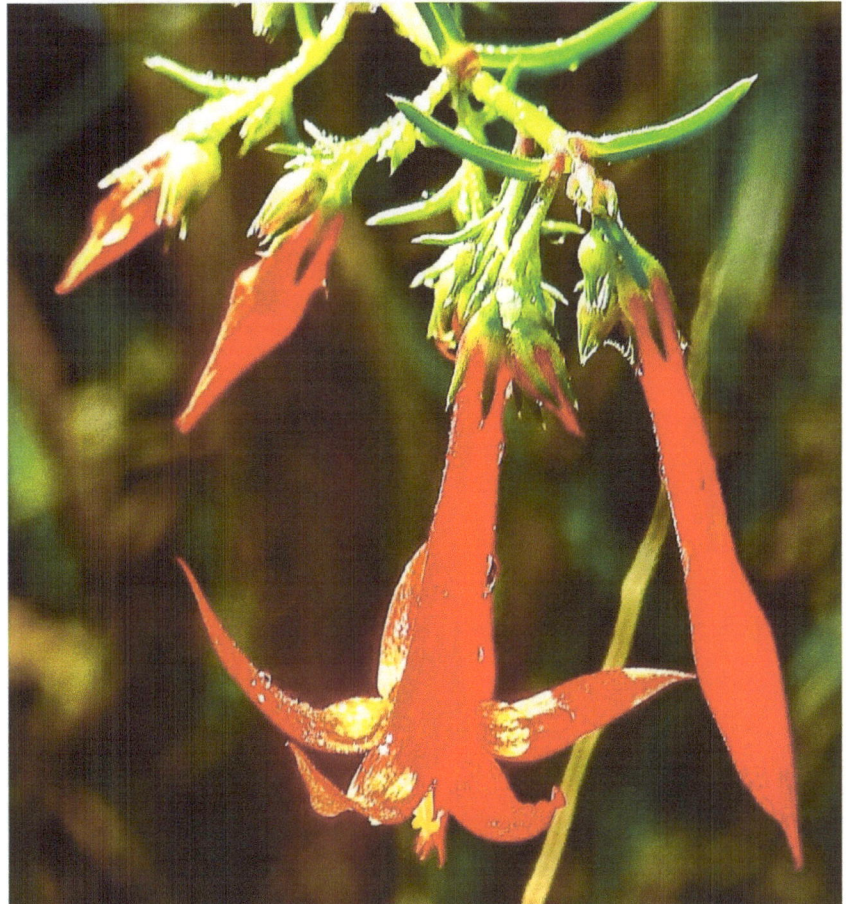

As this picture of a clump of Scarlet Gilia shows, sometimes you cannot get rid of the glare in red pictures. All you can do is work with the contrast, brightness, and lighten and darken settings to get as much detail in the highlights as possible.

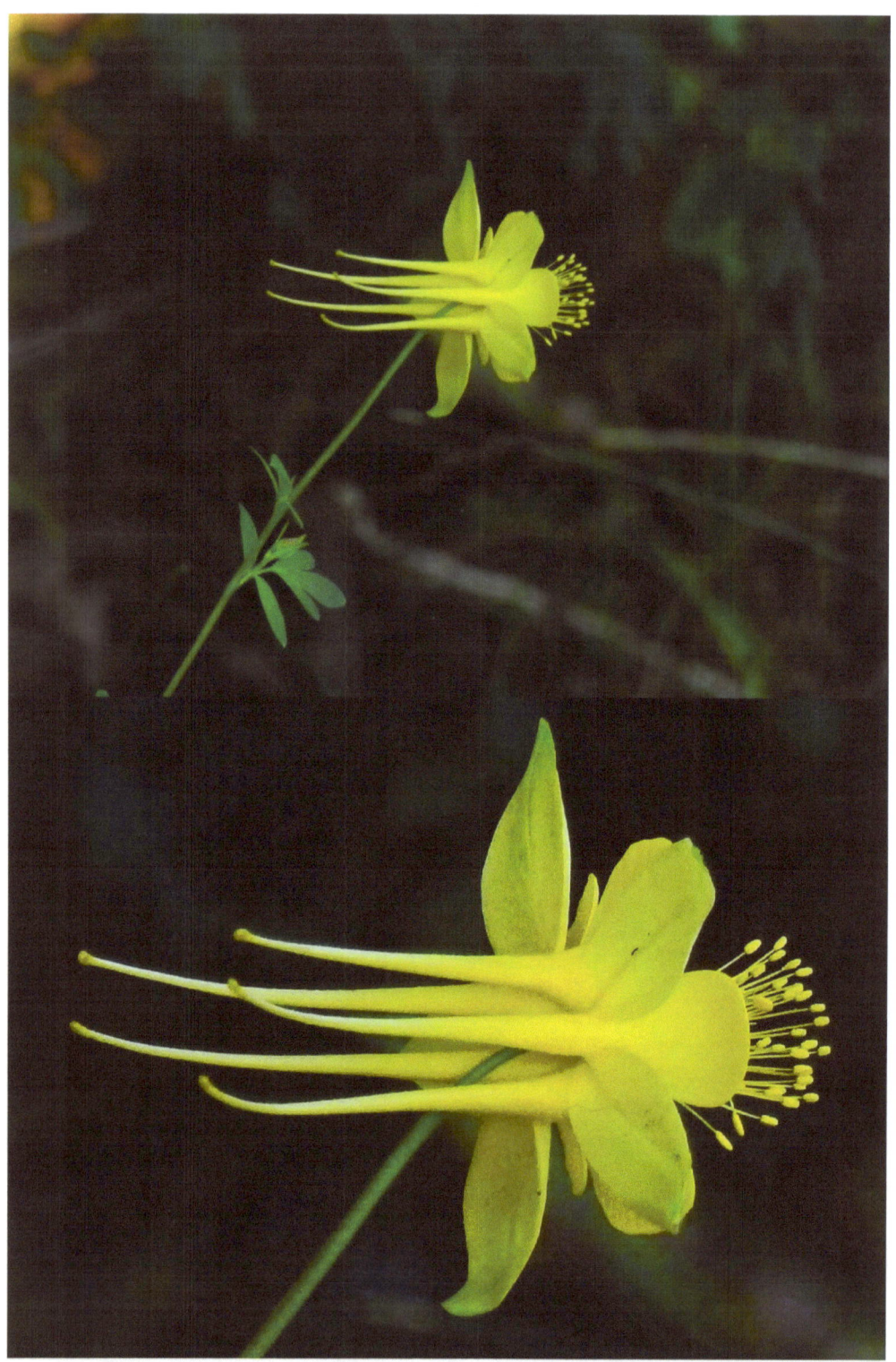

This Yellow Columbine picture is another demonstration of how desirable a dark background, close cropping and adding saturated color are. The close cropping removes distractions. The dark background means that not only will the subject stand out, but that the added saturated color will emphasize both the background and the subject.

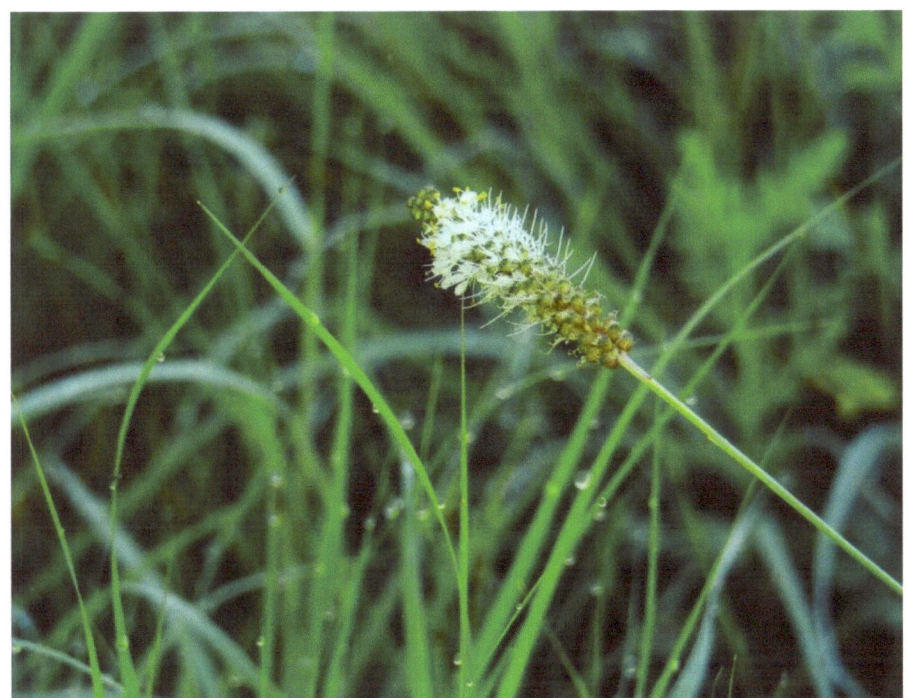

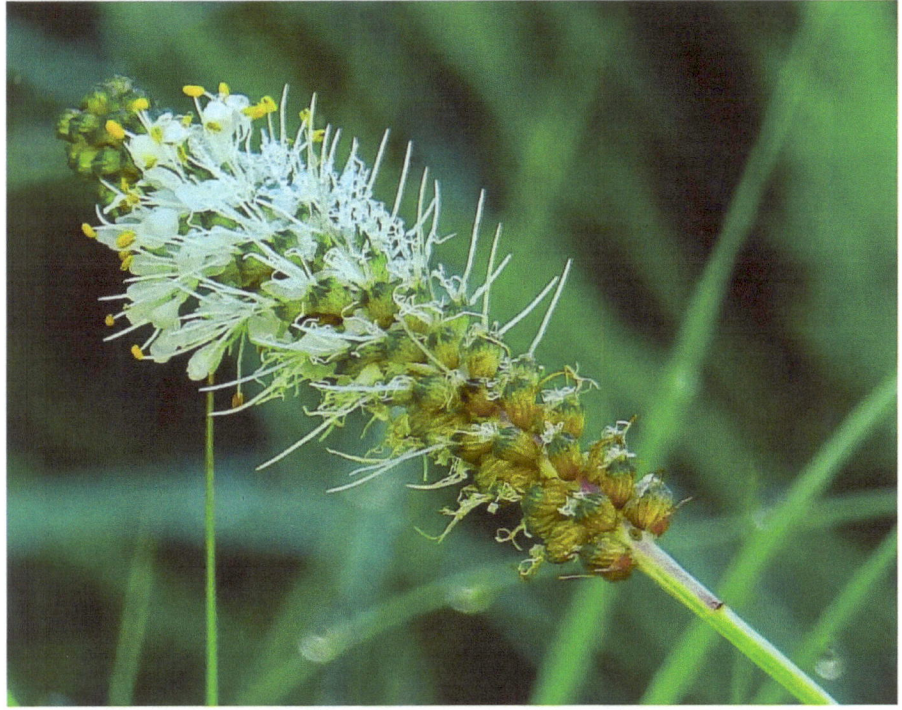

White Prairie Clover prefers to grow amid grasses. This makes it difficult to find a setting with a dark background. Consequently, it is best to utilize the fore-, middle- and background technique. I cut down the contrast to de-emphasize the background and middle-ground and darkened the picture overall. The application of saturated color adds the finishing touch.

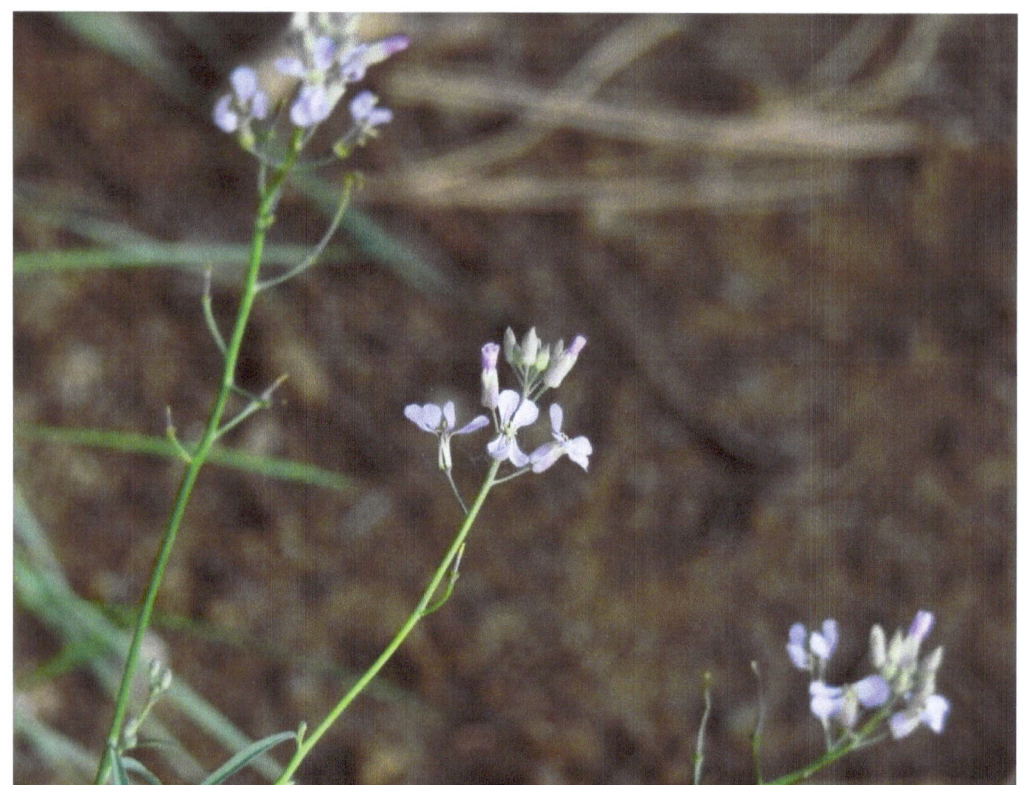

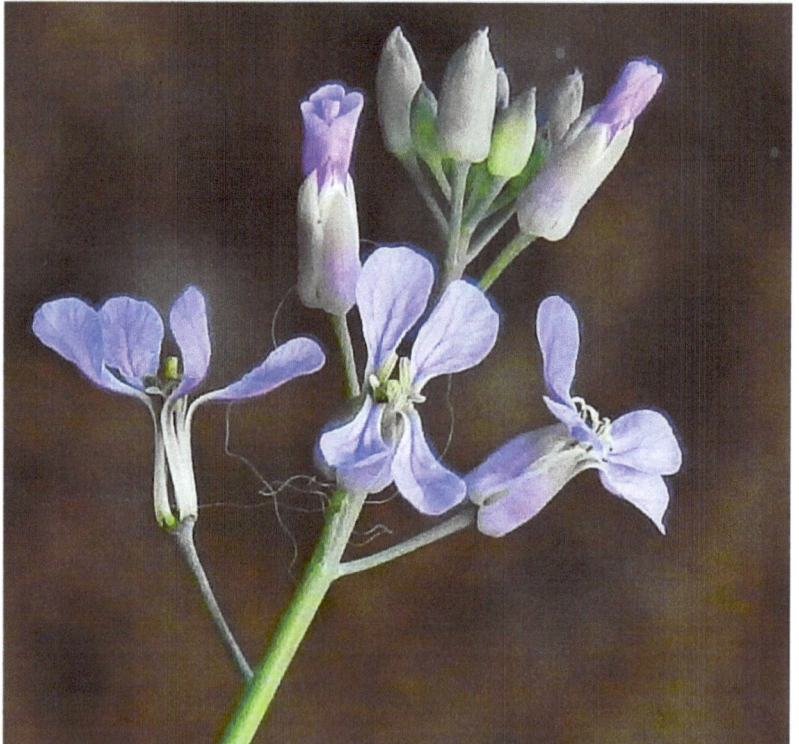

Slimleaf Plainsmustard has an exceptionally tiny flower. It is nearly impossible to get an exceptional picture without extensive re-working the original image. Every previously described action except decreasing the contrast was used in obtaining the final image.

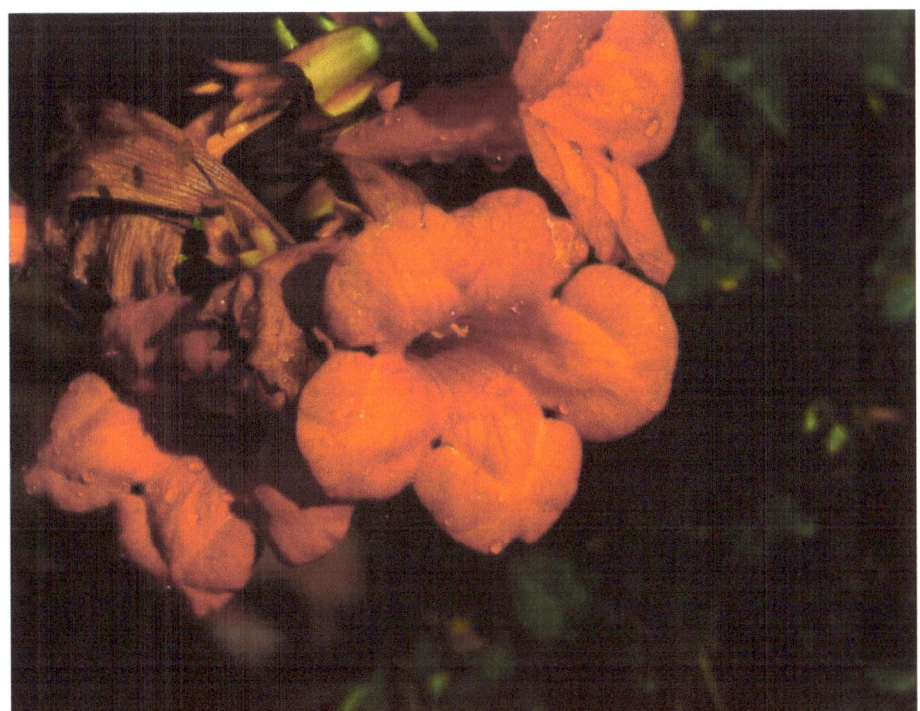

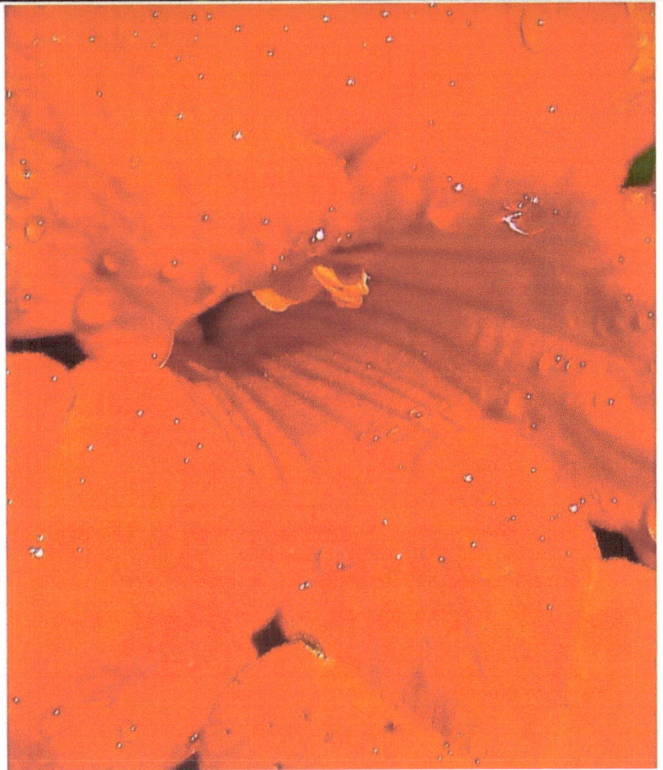

Trumpetvine blooms over an extended period of time. Consequently, it is difficult to get a good original image without wilted flowers appearing somewhere. Extremely close cropping produces an abstract image. Note too how it emphasizes the dew drops. Water droplets are an asset in flower photography.

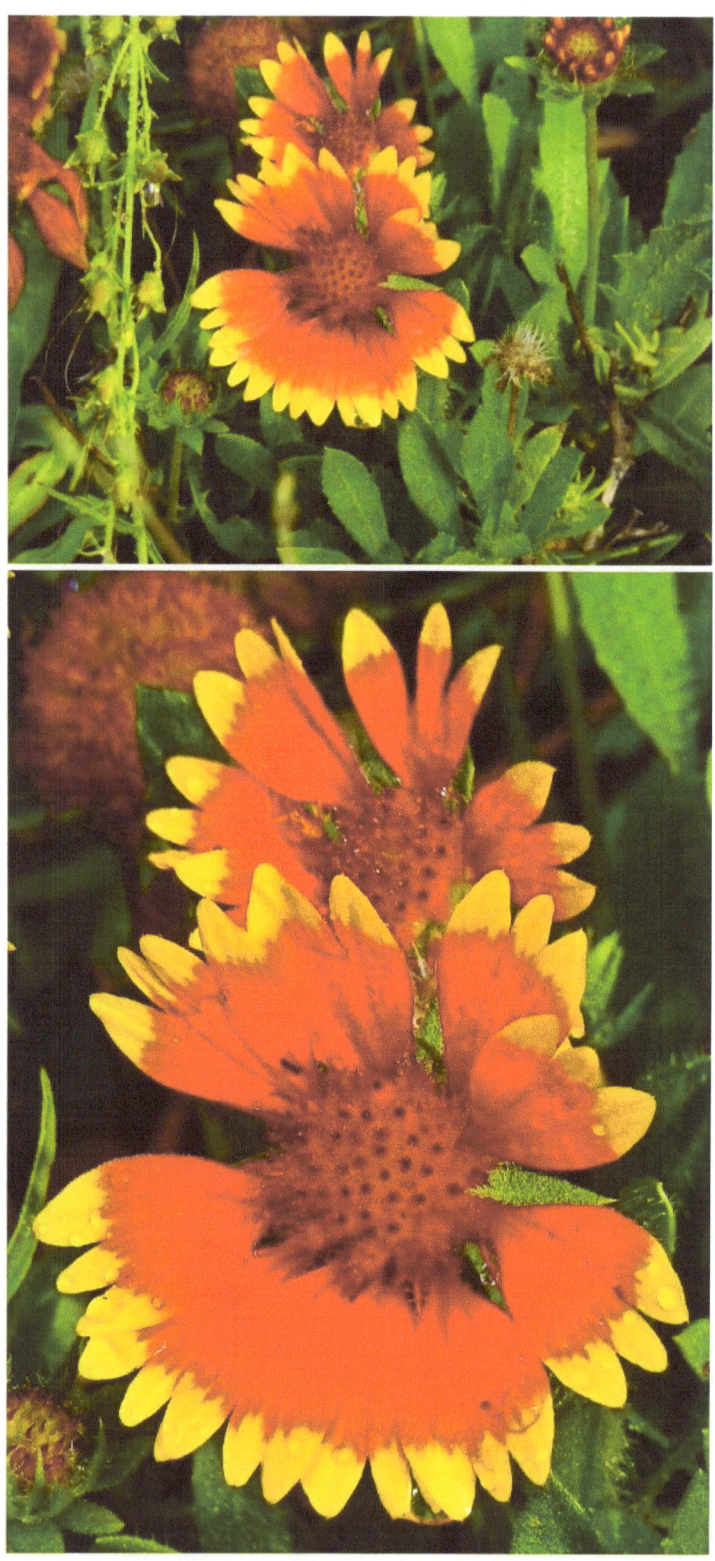

The flowers of a Gaillardia are usually symmetrical like its relative, the sunflower. This unusual composition comes from two unusually-shaped blooms. This is another example of close cropping and the addition of saturated color making the difference between "That's nice" and "WOW".

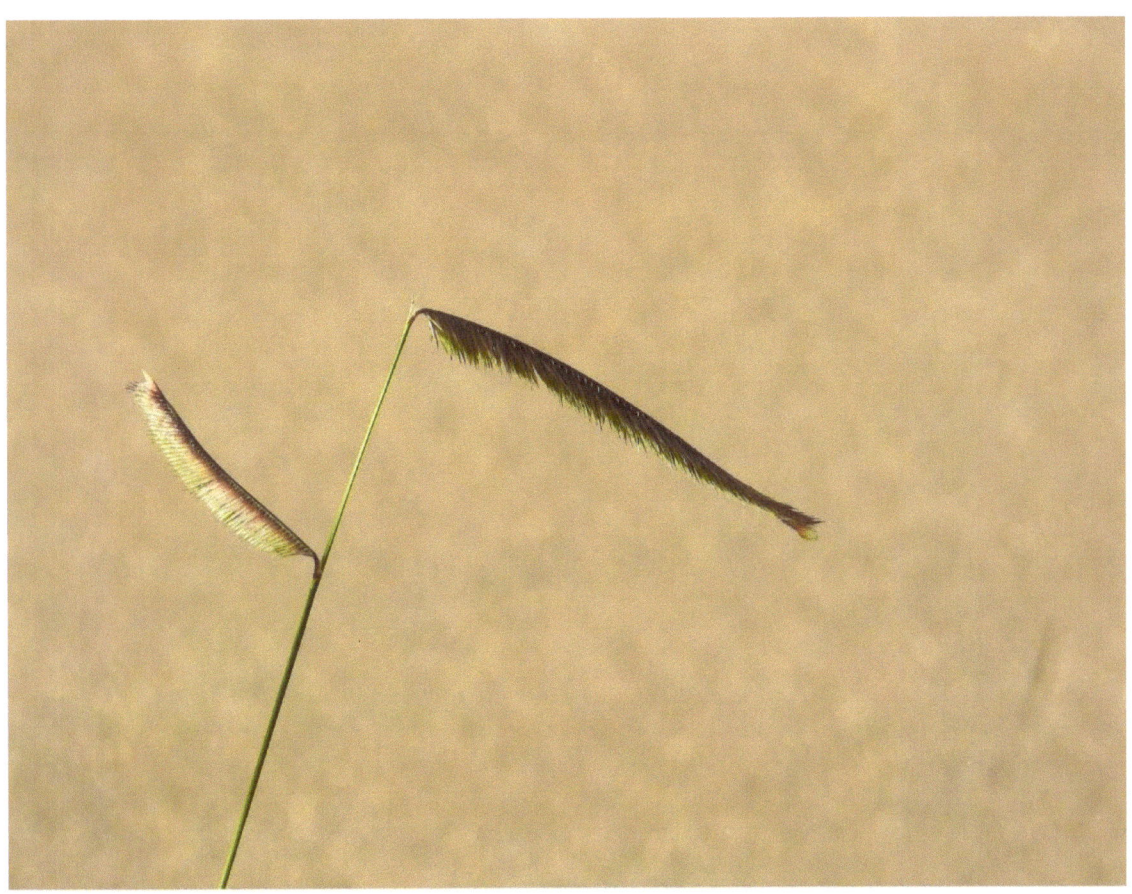

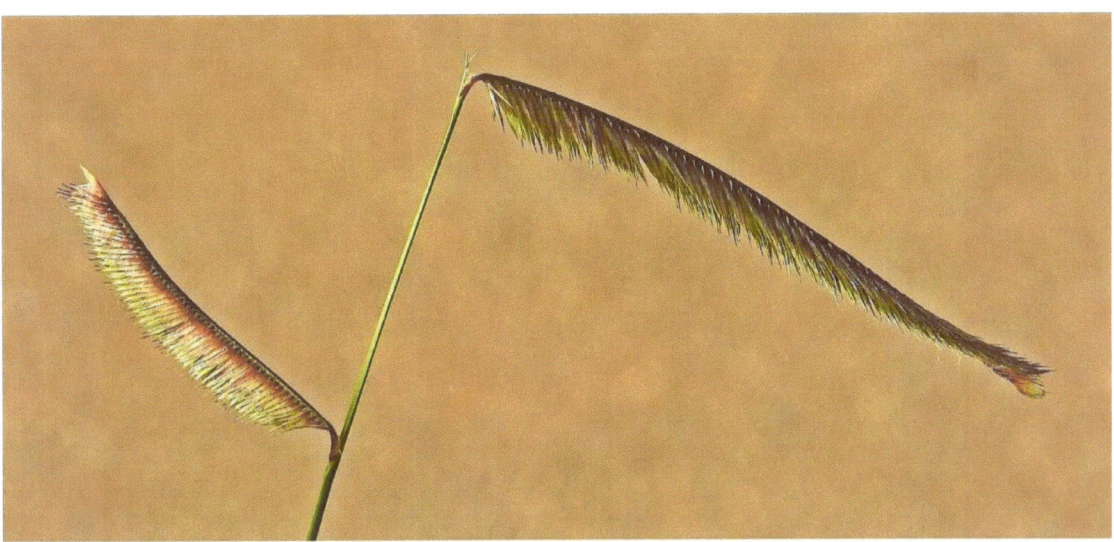

Blue Grama Grass is great for minimalist photography lovers. Here I made use of a sidewalk to provide and absolutely bland background. There is not much change from the original except that individual seeds are slightly more distinguishable.

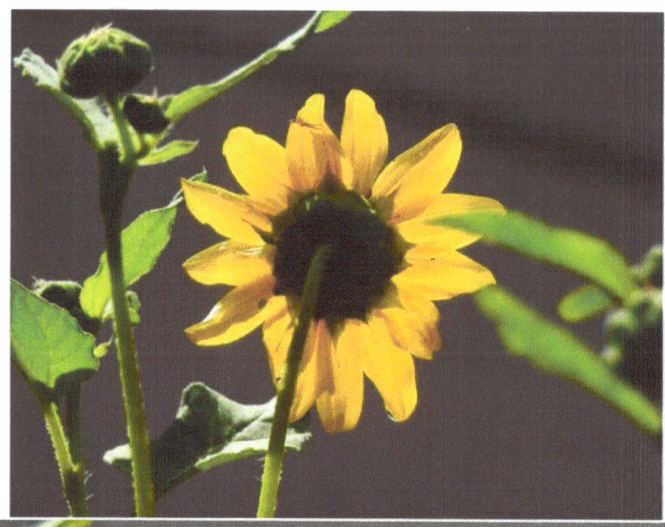

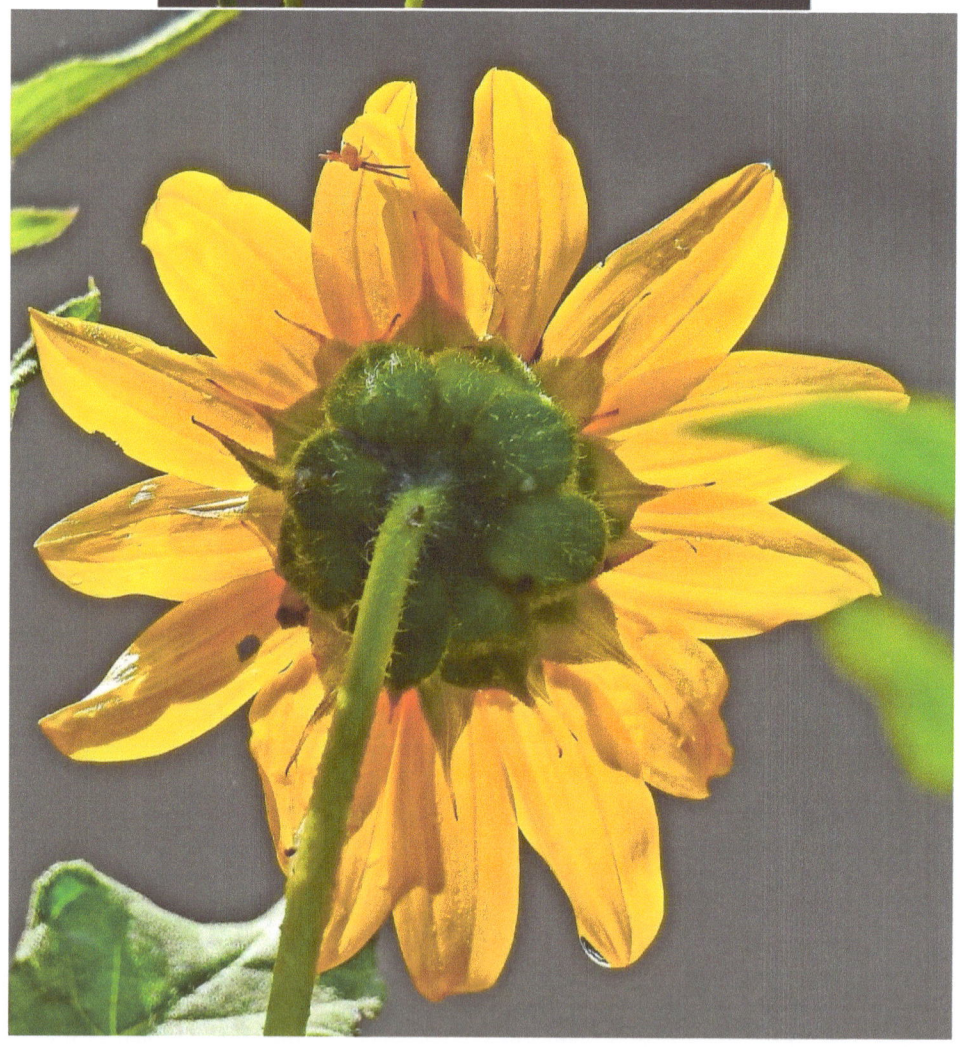

A sunflower offers the chance to photograph from unusual perspectives. Most viewers will instantly recognize the species but few will have looked at it from this angle. Plan your photos just as a painter plans a painting. Shooting with the sun over your shoulder gets tiresome. Face the sun.

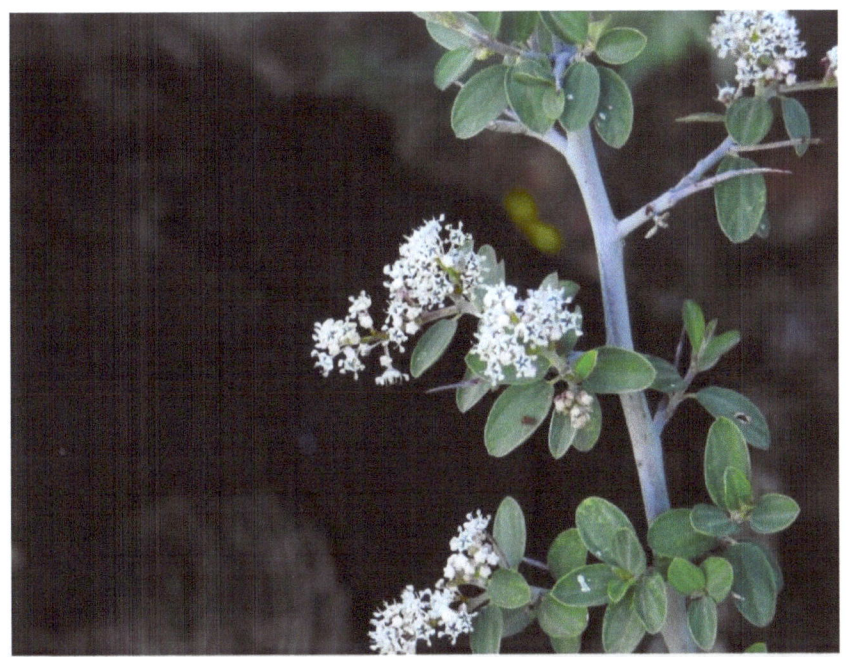

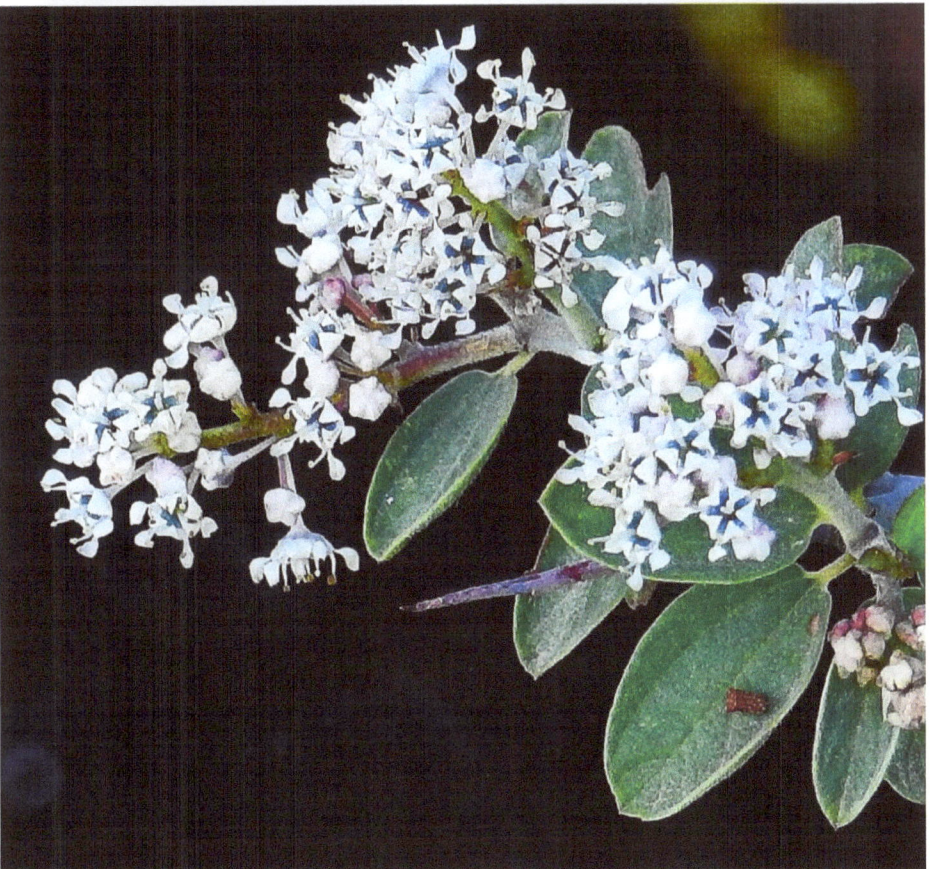

The myriad of small flowers and the fact that each plant has dozens of clusters make Buckbrush hard to photograph. I found an unusual lone cluster right over a burned stump that I used for a background. I like the diagonal formed by the green leaves.

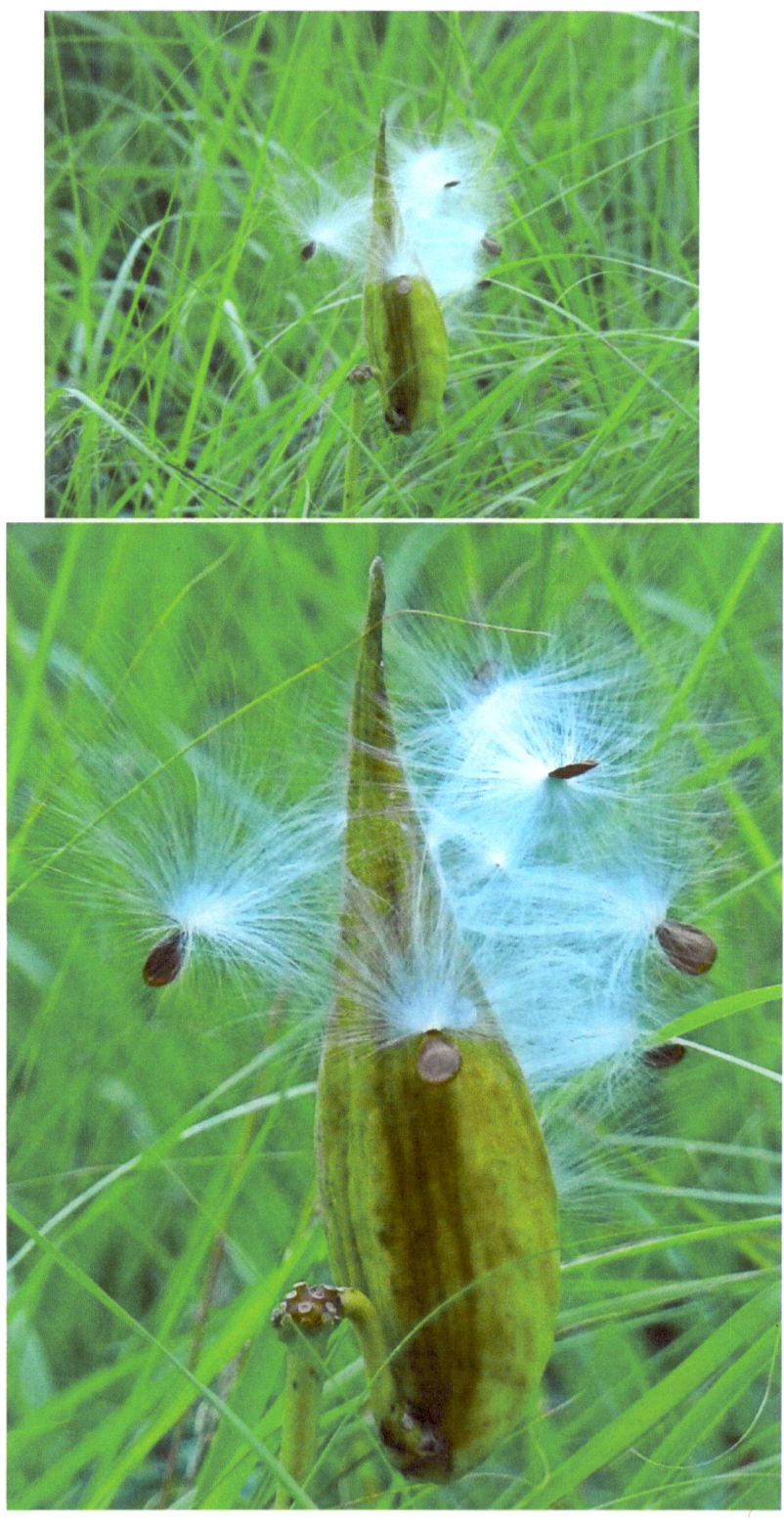

Even on a calm day, a Milkweed dispersing its seeds conveys a sense of energy.

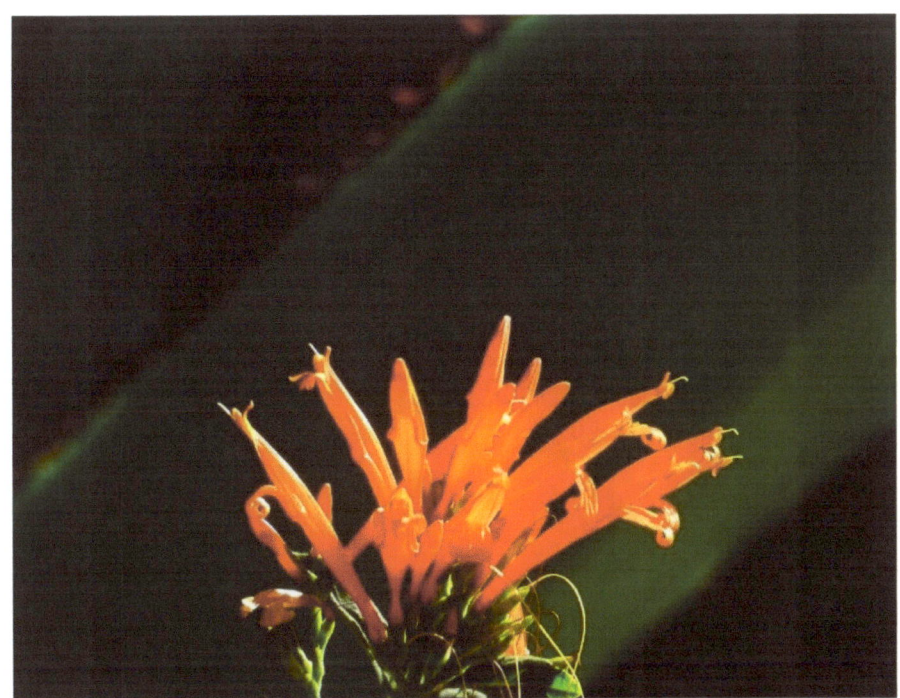

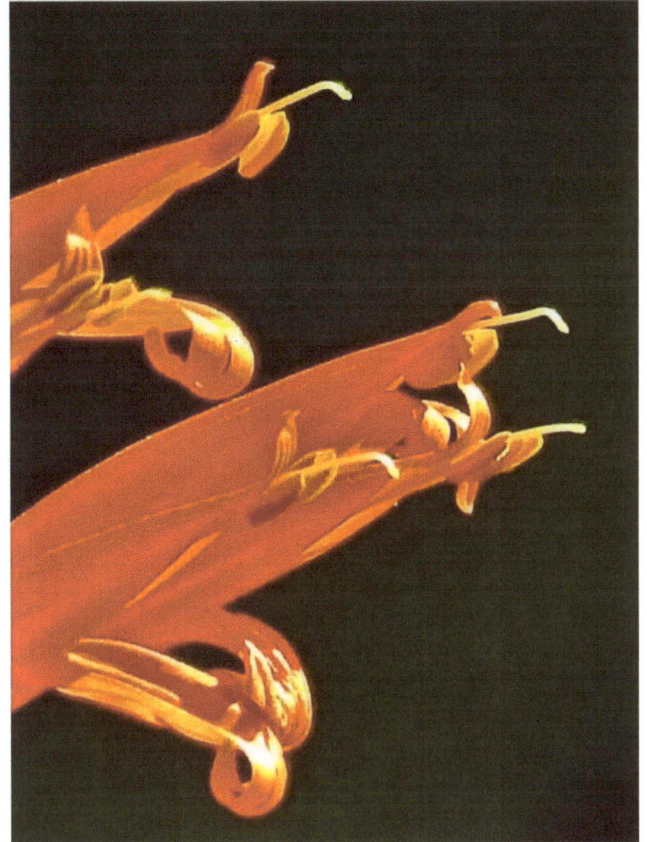

The curls on the petals of this Mexican Honeysuckle are all but unnoticeable in the original picture. However, after some extreme cropping, they are the highlight of the finished product.

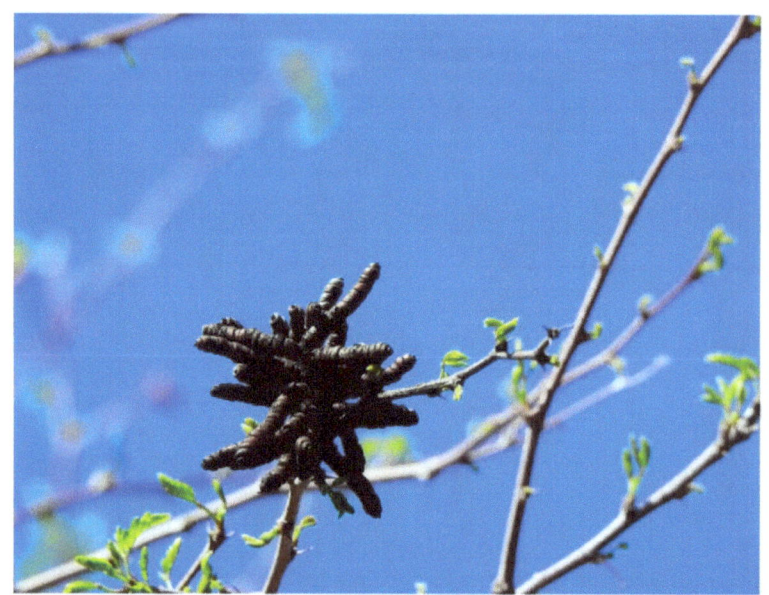

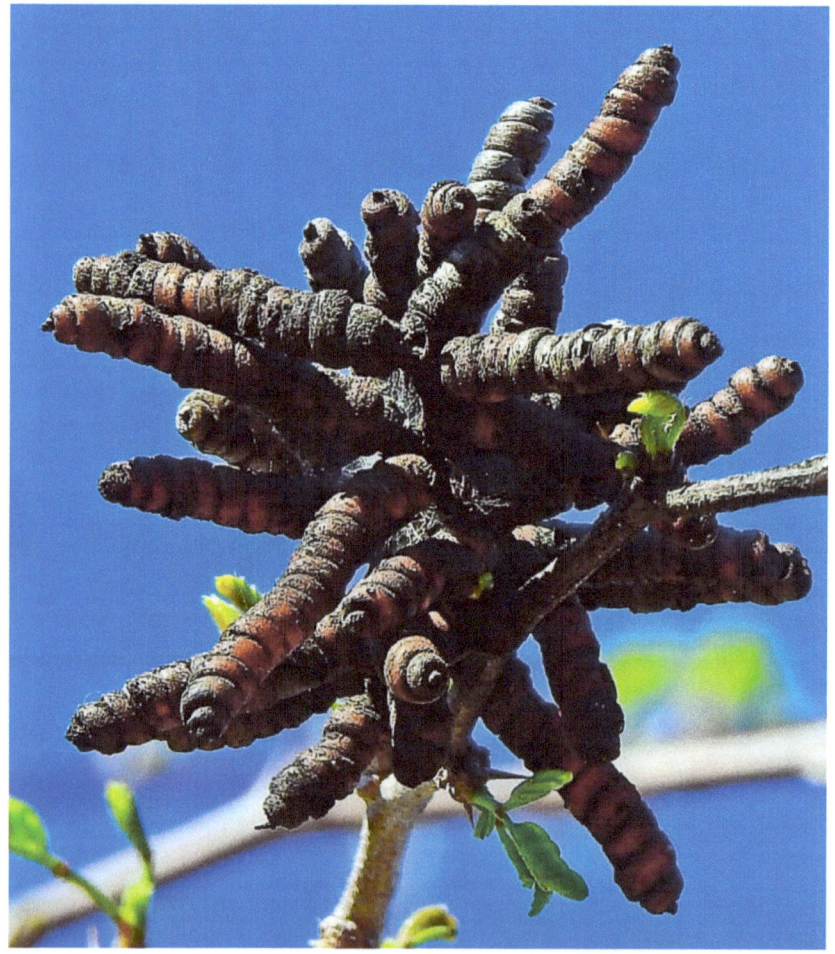

To get the other-worldly appearance of this Screwbean Mesquite seed pod, I lightened the shadows. This was possible with the blue sky background.

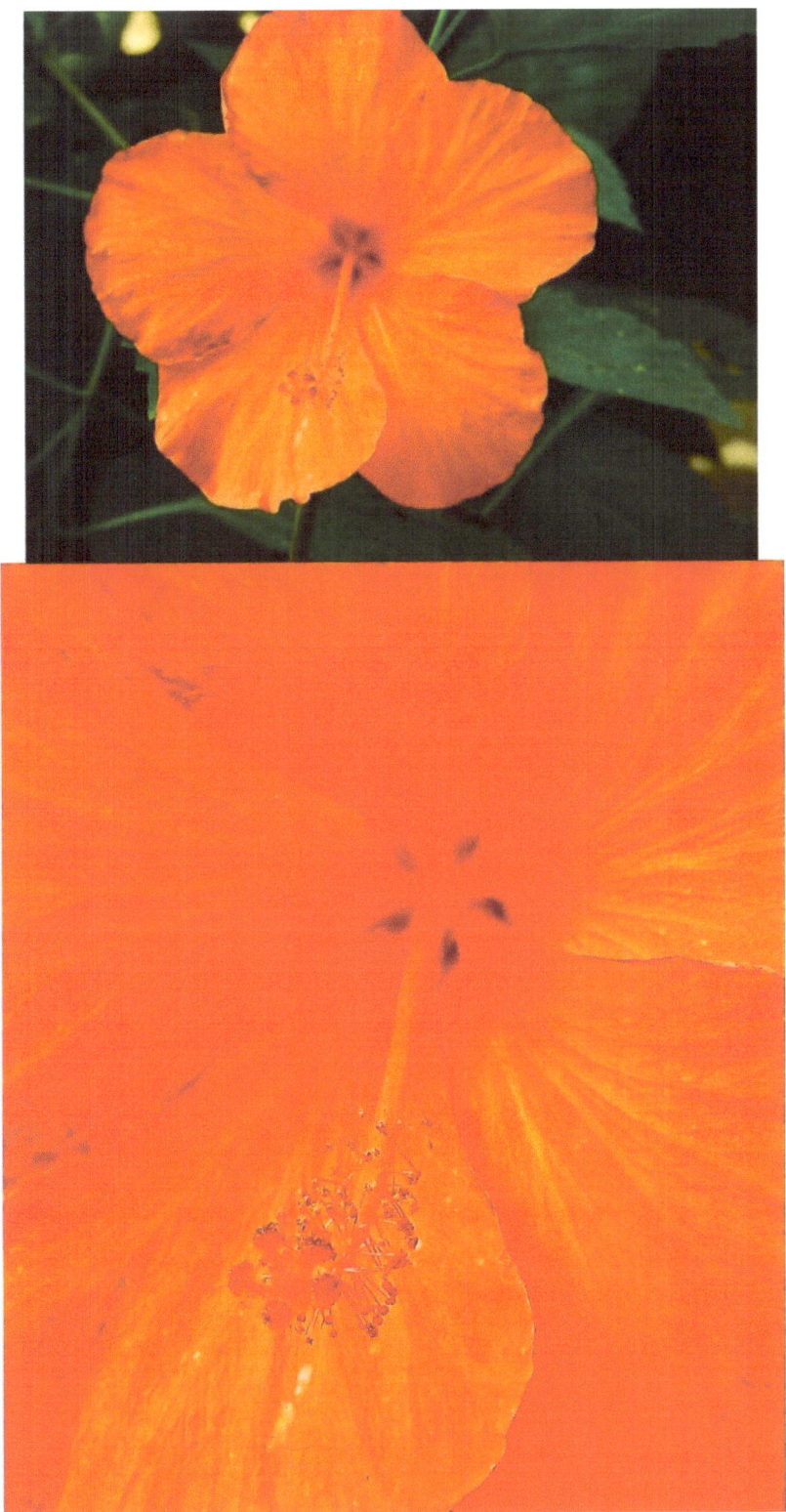

In the original picture of this Hibiscus, I accidently cut off the top of the petals. A useful, abstract picture was salvaged by extreme cropping.

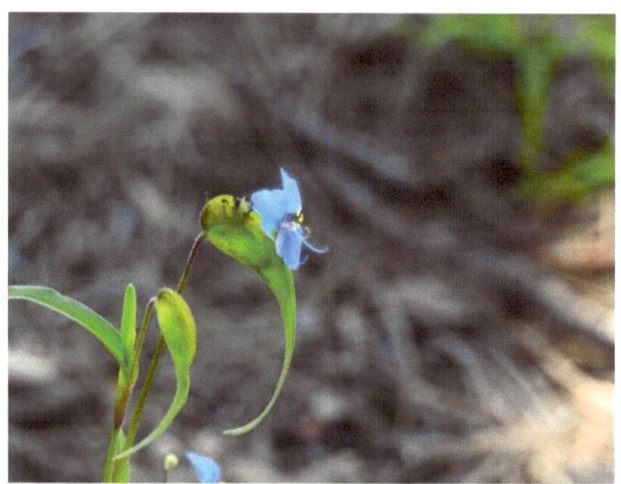

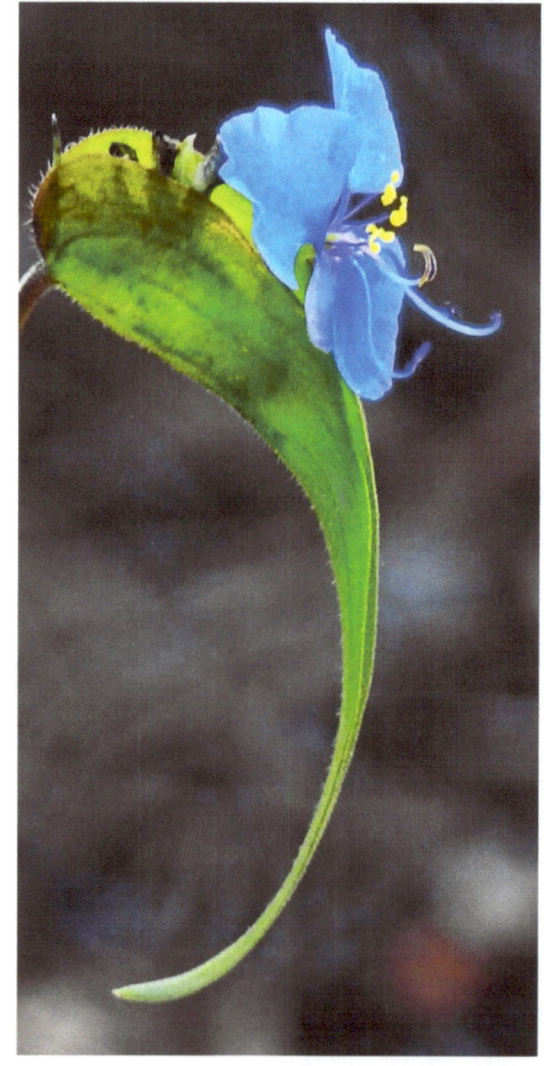

You have to be out early in the morning to get a picture of a Western Dayflower. They bloom at sunrise and are mostly wilted away by noon. A tight crop showing only the bloom would have been another possibility.

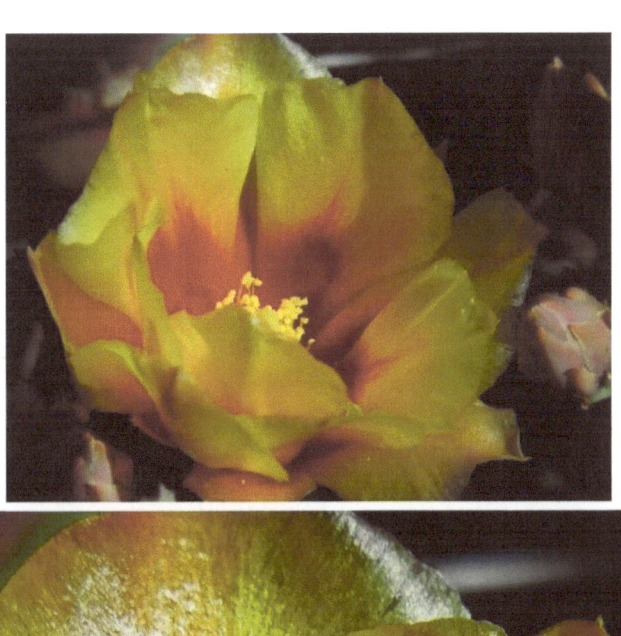

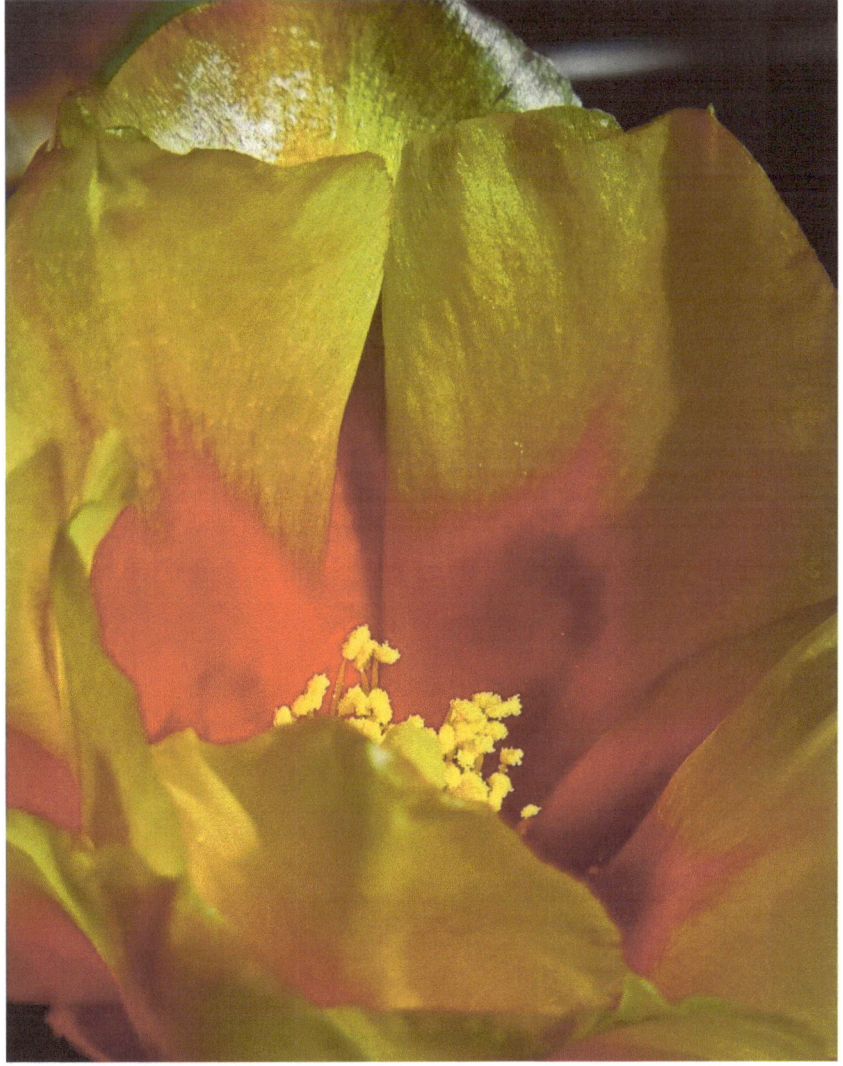

The yellow and red of a Prickly Pear Cactus bloom make it appear as if the blossom itself is the source of light

OTHER BOOKS BY AL LODWICK

The Homeschool Resource Series

Introduction to Birds

Gambel's Quail

Decisions for Preschoolers

The Preschooler's A-B-Cs of Nature

The Preschooler's Nature Book

Reference Photos For Nature Artists

Abert's Squirrels

Acorn Woodpeckers

Arizona Wildflowers

Bald Eagles

Cooper's Hawks

Double-crested Cormorants

Great Blue-Herons

Sedona: 50 Memorable Landscapes

Snakes and Lizards

Travel Guides

Grand Canyon National Park: The Roadtrip Guide

Highlights of The Highlands Center and Lynx Lake Area of Arizona: A Naturalist's View

Biblical

The Creation Story: King James Version with Photographs

Pharmacy Practice

Expand Your Pharmacy Practice: Become an Expert Witness or Litigation Consultant

Novel With Scott Mies

Murder or Pestle

www.ingramcontent.com/pod-product-compliance
Lightning Source LLC
Chambersburg PA
CBHW050423180526
45159CB00005B/2389